ISLA NEGRA

ISLA NEGRA

POEMS BY PABLO NERUDA

Edited by
Dennis Maloney

Translated by
Maria Jacketti, Dennis Maloney, and Clark Zlotchew

WHITE PINE PRESS · BUFFALO, NEW YORK

White Pine Press
P.O. Box 236, Buffalo, New York 14201

Publication of this book was made possible by grants from
the Chrysopolae Foundation,
the National Endowment for the Arts,
and by public funds from the
New York State Council on the Arts, a state agency.

Printed and bound in the United States of America.

Book design: Elaine LaMattina

Cover photograph:
"Neruda entrando al bar de su casa en Isla Negra"
by Alicia D'Amico.

Isla Negra

SEAQUAKE

THE HOUSE IN THE SAND

TRANSLATED BY
DENNIS MALONEY & CLARK ZLOTCHEW

The Sea

The Pacific Ocean was overflowing the borders of the map. There was no place to put it. It was so large, wild and blue that it didn't fit anywhere. That's why it was left in front of my window.

The humanists worried about the little men it devoured over the years.

They do not count.

Not even that galleon, laden with cinnamon and pepper that perfumed it as it went down.

No.

Not even the explorers' ship—fragile as a cradle dashed to pieces in the abyss—which keeled over with its starving men.

No.

In the ocean, a man dissolves like a bar of salt. And the water doesn't know it.

The Key

I lost my key, my hat, my head! The key came from Raul's
general store in Temuco. It was outside, immense, lost, pointing
out the general store, "The Key," to the Indians. When I came
north I asked Raul for it, I tore it from him, I stole it in the
midst of fierce and stormy winds. I carried it off toward Loncoche
on horseback. From there the key, like a bride dressed in white,
accompanied me on the night train.

I have come to realize that everything I misplace in the house
is carried off by the sea. The sea seeps in at night through key-
holes, underneath and over the tops of doors and windows.

Since by night, in the darkness, the sea is yellow, I suspected,
without verifying, its secret invasion. On the umbrella stand or
on the gentle ears of Maria Celeste, I would discover drops of
metallic sea, atoms of its golden mask. The sea is dry at night. It
retains its dimension, its power, and its swells, but turns into a
great goblet of sonorous air, into an ungraspable volume that has
rid itself of its waters. It enters my house to find out what and
how much I have. It enters by night, before dawn: everything in
the house is still and salty, the plates, the knives, the things
scrubbed by contact with its wildness lose nothing, but become
frightened when the sea enters with all its cat-yellow eyes.

That is how I lost my key, my hat, my head.

They were carried off by the ocean in its swaying motion. I
found them on a new morning. They are returned to me by the
harbinger wave that deposits lost things at my door.

In this way, by a trick of the sea, the morning has returned to
me my white key, my sand-covered hat, my head—the head of a
shipwrecked sailor.

The Agates

Where do these agates come from into my hands? Each morning they appear at my doorstep, and it is an early-morning scramble, since some stray shepherd from inland, either Gonzáles Vera, or Lina or Maria fights over these small translucent stones with the Yankas, shellfish gatherers by trade, who, at the edge of the sea, lay in wait for merchandise and think they are entitled to whatever the tide casts ashore.

The truth is that they always wake me at dawn, and here again is the treasure the sea sends me, alone in its hands, at so much per stone or per hundred stones or per kilo or per barrel.

And in my hand the mysterious drops of round light, the color of honey or of oyster, resembling petrified grapes in order to fit into Espinosa's poem about the Genil River, softly sprinkled by some ashen deity, at times bored through the center by some golden spur, undermined by the tiniest of waves: agates of Isla Negra, mist-colored or light blue, softly carmine or deep green, or violet or reddish or variegated on the inside like clusters of muscat grapes: and often static with transparency, open to the light surrendered by the honeycomb of the ocean to the whim of the crystal: to purity itself.

The House

The house... I don't know when this was born in me... It was in the mid-afternoon, we were on the way to those lonely places on horseback... Don Eladio was in front, fording the Cordoba stream which had swollen... For the first time I felt the pang of this smell of winter at the sea, a mixture of sweet herbs and salty sand, seaweed and thistle.

The People

Just as I've always thought of myself as a carpenter-poet, I think of Rafita as the poet of carpentry. He brings his tools wrapped in a newspaper, under his arm, and unwraps what looks to me like a chapter and picks up the worn handles of his hammers and rasps, losing himself in the wood. His work is perfect.

A little boy and a dog accompany him and watch his hands as they move in careful circles. His eyes are like those of Saint John of the Cross, and his hands raise the colossal tree trunks with delicacy as well as skill.

On the rauli wood beams, I wrote with chalk the names of dead friends, and he went along carving my calligraphy into the wood as swiftly as if he had flown behind me and written the names again with the tip of a wing.

The Names

I didn't write them on the roof-beams because they were famous, but because they were companions.

Rojas Giménez, the nomad, nocturnal, pierced with the grief of farewells, dead with joy, pigeon breeder, madman of the shadows.

Joaquín Cifuentes, whose verses rolled like stones in the river.

Federico, who made me laugh like no one else could and who put us all in mourning for a century.

Paul Eluard, whose forget-me-not color eyes are as sky-blue as always and retain their blue strength beneath the earth.

Miguel Hernández, whistling to me like a nightingale from the trees on Princesa Street until they caged my nightingale.

Nazim, noisy bard, brave gentleman, friend.

Why did they leave so soon? Their names will not slip down from the rafters. Each one of them was a victory. Together they were the sum of my light. Now, a small anthology of my sorrows.

The Medusa

They hid me in Valparaiso. Those were turbulent days and my poetry circulated in the street. This disturbed the Sinister One. He demanded my head.

It was in the hills above the port. The boys arrived during the afternoon. Sailors without a ship. What had they seen in the habor? They would tell me everything.

From my hiding place, I could see only through the glass medium of the lofty window. It looked out over an alley.

The news was that an old ship had broken down. Does it have a figurehead on the prow, I anxiously asked.

Of course it has a *mona*, the boys said. A *mona*, or *mono*, which in ordinary Spanish is a monkey, is for Chileans the term for any kind of statue.

From that moment on I directed the activities from the shadows. Since it was very difficult to take her down, she would be given to whomever carried her off.

But the figurehead was to share my destiny. She was very large, and she had to be hidden. Where? At last, the boys found an anonymous and spacious shed. There she was buried in a corner while I crossed the mountains on horseback.

When I came back from exile, years later, the shed had been sold (perhaps along with my lady-friend). We searched for her. She was proudly erected in someone's garden inland. No one any longer knew whose she was or what she was.

It was as hard to take her out of the garden as it had been to take her out of the sea. Solimano brought her to me one morning in an immense truck. With great effort we unloaded her and left her leaning on the stone bench with her face to the ocean.

I didn't know her. I had directed the entire operation on the wreck from my darkness. Then violence separated us; later, the land did.

Now I saw her, covered with so many coats of paint that neither the ears nor the nose could be seen. She certainly was majestic in her flowing tunic. She reminded me of Gabriela Mistral, when I, a small child, met her in Temuco, when she would walk around wrapped in Franciscan robes from her topknot to her overshoes.

The Anchor

The anchor arrived from Antofagasta. From some very large ship, the kind that hauls potassium nitrate across the seven seas. It was sleeping there in the arid sands of the great North. One day it occurred to someone to send it to me. With its great size and weight it was a difficult voyage, from truck to crane, from ship to train, to harbor, to ship. When it arrived at my door, it refused to move any further. They brought a tractor. The anchor didn't budge. They brought several oxen, which dragged it along in a short, frantic run, and then it did move, to remain leaning against the plants in the sand.

"Will you paint it? It's rusting."

It doesn't matter. It is powerful and silent as though it were still on its vessel and the corrosive wind was not attacking it in all its fury. I like the dross that little by little is covering it with infinite scales of orange iron.

Everyone ages in his or her own way, and the anchor bears up in solitude as it did on its vessel, with dignity. One hardly notes the flaked-off iron on its arms.

Love for This Book

In these lonely regions I have been powerful,
like a fine set of tools,
like untrammeled grass which lets loose its seed,
or like a dog rolling around in the dew.
Matilde, time will pass wearing out and inflaming
other skin, other fingernails, other eyes, and then
the algae that lashed our wild rocks,
the waves that build, ceaselessly, their whiteness,
all will be steady without us,
all will be ready for the new days,
with no idea of our destiny.

What do we leave here but the lost cry
of the seabird in the winter sand, in the gusts of wind
that cut our faces and kept us
upright in the light of purity,
as in the heart of an illustrious star?

What do we leave, living like a nest
of surly birds, alive, among the thickets
or static, perched on the frigid cliffs?
So then, if living was nothing more than anticipating
the earth, this soil and its harshness,
deliver me, my love, from not doing my duty, and help me
return to my place beneath the hungry earth.

We asked the ocean for its rose,
its open star, its bitter contact,
and to the overburdened, the fellow man, the wounded

we gave the freedom gathered in the wind.
It's late now. Perhaps
it was only a long day the color of honey and blue,
perhaps only a night, like the eyelid
of a grave look that encompassed
the measure of the sea that surrounded us,
and in this territory we found only a kiss,
only ungraspable love that will remain here
wandering among sea foam and roots.

THE STONES OF CHILE

Translated by
Dennis Maloney

Some Words for a Book of Stone

This stony book, born in the desolate coastlands and mountain ranges of my country, was abandoned in my thoughts for twenty years. It wasn't possible to write it then for wandering reasons and the tasks of every year and day.

It is the poet who must sing with his countrymen and give to man all that is man: dream and love, light and night, reason and madness. But let's not forget the stones! We should never forget the silent castles, the bristling, round gifts of the planet. They fortify citadels, advance to kill or die, adorn our existence without compromise, preserving the mysteries of their ultraterrestrial matter, independent and eternal.

My compatriot, Gabriela Mistral, said once that in Chile it is the skeleton that one sees first, the profusion of rocks in the mountains and sand. As nearly always, there is much truth in what she said.

I came to live in Isla Negra in 1939 and the coast was strewn with these extraordinary presences of stone and they spoke to me in a hoarse and drenching language, a jumble of marine cries and primal warnings.

Because of this, the book, adorned with portraits of creatures of stone, is a conversation that I open to all the poets of the earth, so that it may be continued by all in order to encounter the secret of stone and of life.

—Pablo Neruda

History

For stone was the blood,
for stone the weeping,
the prayer, the procession:
stone was free will.

Because in sweat and in fire
the gods of stone were born
and then the saint of rain grew,
the lord of the struggles
for the corn, for the earth,
bird gods, serpent gods,
the fertile, the unfortunate,
all were born of stone:
America raised them
with a thousand small golden hands,
with eyes already lost,
clouded with blood and neglect.

But my country was of light,
a man alone came and went,
without other gods than thunder:

and there my heart grew:
I came from Araucania.

It was plant and seashore,
diurnal like the hummingbirds,
red like the crab,
green as water in October,

silvery as a small fish,
wild as a partridge,
and thinner than an arrow
was the southern land, worn away
by the great winds of the sky,
by the stars of the sea.

In Chile gods are not born,
Chile is the home of quarries.
So, in the rock grew
arms and mouths, feet and hands,
the stone became a monument:
it cut open the cold, the month of June
added petals and feathers
and then time came and arrived,
left and returned, returned and left,
until it deserted,
the kingdom without blood and without gods,
filled with pure figures:

Stone illuminated my country
with its natural statues.

The Bull

The oldest bull crossed the day.
His legs scratched the planet.
He continued, traveling to where the sea lives.
He reached the shore, the oldest bull.
On the edge of time, the ocean.
He closed his eyes and grass covered him.
He breathed the whole green distance.
And silence built the rest.

The Dead Sailor

The sailor wounded
by the seas,
fell into the ancient abyss,
into the sargasso's dream.
Immediately, he was hurled down
from wind
and the furious salt
scattered his death.

Here is his head.

The stone preserved his scars
when the hard
night
wore away his body. Now he remains.

And a sea plant kisses his wound.

The Shipwrecked

Shipwrecks of stone sang on the coast
and the tower they sang was radiant salt
raising itself drop by drop until it turned into water,
bubble by bubble climbing to the air.

The shipwrecked that oblivion turned to stone
(not an oblivion but all the oblivion),
those that hoped, partly submerged, for
earthly help, voices, shoulders, wine, aspirin,
and only received infernal crabs,
they became the stiff dead ones with granite eyes
and here their statues were scattered,
their formless, round, solitary statues.

Yet they learned to sing. Slowly
the voice of all the shipwrecked rose.
It was a song of salt like a wave,
it was a lighthouse of invisible stones:
parallel stones
looking toward the lightning bolts of oceania
toward the bristling sea,
toward the infinite without boats or countries.

A sun fell, lifting
the green sword of its last light,
another sun fell beneath
from cloud to cloud toward winter,
still another sun
crossed the waves,

savage plumes
that lifted anger and seafoam
over the irritated
walls of turquoise
and there in the huge mass:
parallel sisters,
immobile,
detained
by the rest of the cold,
clustered within its force
like lionesses transformed into rock,
like prows that go on without ocean
in the direction of the time,
the crystalline eternity of the journey.

Solitudes

Among the stones of the coast, walking,
by the shore of Chile,
farther off
sea and sea, moon and sea grass,
the lonely expanse of the planet.

The coast broken
by thunder,
consumed
by the teeth of every dawn,
worn by great stirrings
of weather and waves:
slow birds circle
with iron-colored feathers
and they know the world ends here.
No one said why,
no one exists,
it isn't written, there are no numbers or letters,
no one trampled the sand, dark
as pollen of lead.
here desolate flowers were born,
plants that expressed themselves with thorns
and sudden blossoms
of furious petals.
No one said there wasn't any territory,
that here emptiness begins,
the ancient emptiness that guides
with catastrophe, darkness
and shadow, darkness, shadows:

so it is the harsh coast, that road
of south and north and west, and solitude.

Beautiful virtue of that struggle
water and seafoam erect
on this long border:
a structure like a flower-wave
repeating its castle-like form,
its tower that decays and crumbles
only to swell beating anew
pretending
to populate the darkness with its beauty,
fill the abyss with light.
Walking
from the final antarctic
by stone and sea, hardly
saying a word,
only the eyes speak and rest.

Innumerable solitude swept
by wind and salt, by cold,
by chains,
by moon and seaquake:
I must recall the toothless star
that here collapsed,
to gather the fragments
of stone, to hear
no one and speak with no one,
to be and not be a solitary motion:
I am the sentinel
of a barracks without soldiers,
of a great solitude filled with stones.

The Stones of Chile

Mad stones of Chile, pouring
from mountain ranges,
full of rocks
black, blind, opaque,
that joined
roads to the earth,
that placed time and stone
by the day's journey,
white rocks
that interrupt the rivers
and are kissed
smooth
by a seismic
ribbon of seafoam,
granite
of the glimmering
high seas
beneath
the snow
like a monastery,
backbone
of the
strongest
country
or unmovable
ship,
prow
of the terrible earth,
stone, infinitely pure stone,

sealed
like
a cosmic dove,
stiff from sun, from wind, from energy,
from mineral dream, from dark time,
crazy stones,
stars
and pavilion
slept,
rolling peaks, cliffs:
knew the stillness
around
your lasting silence,
beneath the Antarctic
mantle of Chile,
beneath
your iron clarity.

House

Perhaps this is the house I lived in
when neither I nor earth existed,
when all was moon or stone or darkness,
when still light was unborn.
Perhaps then this stone was
my house, my windows or my eyes.
This rose of granite reminds me
of something that dwelled in me or I in it,
a cave, or cosmic head of dreams,
cup or castle, ship or birth.
I touch the stubborn spirit of rock,
its rampart pounds in the brine,
and my flaws remain here,
wrinkled essence that rose
from the depths to my soul,
and stone I was, stone I will be. Because of this
I touch this stone, and for me it hasn't died:
it's what I was, what I will be, resting
from a struggle long as time.

The Blind Statue

It's been thousands and thousands of
years of stone.
I was a stonecutter
and this is what I did
striking
without hands
or hammer,
piercing
without chisel,
staring into the sun without eyes,
without being,
without existence but in the wind,
with only a wave for my thought,
without tools other
than time,
the time,
the passing time.

I sculpted the statue blind
so that she wouldn't see,
that there
in the desolate
sand
she would keep her mass
like my monument:
the blind
statue
which the first man
that departed from stone,

the son of power,
the first
that dug, touched and imposed on
its lost creation,
searching for fire.

And I was born, naked
and blue, a stonecutter,
lengthwise from shores in darkness
from rivers still unknown
in caves lashed by the tails
of somber lizards,
and it was hard to encounter myself,
to become hands,
eyes, fingers, seeking
my own blood,
and then my joy
became a statue:
my own form that I had copied
striking across the centuries in stone.

Ox

Creature of seafoam
traveling
by night, day,
sand.
Animal
of autumn
walking
toward the ancient
scent of moss,
sweet ox
in whose beard
flowered rocks
of the subsoil,
and where the earthquake armed itself
with thunder and footsteps,
ruminating the darkness,
lost
between lighting flashes
while seafoam lives,
while the day
extracts
the hours from its tower
and the night collapses,
over time
her dark cold sack,
trembling.

The Harp

Only the music came. There was no feather, hair,
milk, smoke or names. Neither night nor day.
Alone between the planets born from the eclipse
music trembled like cloth.
Suddenly fire and cold coagulated in a drop
and the universe molded its extensive display,
lava, bristling ashes, slippery dawn,
everything was transformed from hardness to hardness,
and under the dampness newly celestial,
established the diamond with its frozen symmetry.
Then the primal sound,
the solitary music of the world
congealed and fell changing into a star,
a harp, a zither, silence, stone.

Along the Chilean coast, with cold and winter,
when rain falls washing the weeks.
Listen: solitude becomes music once more,
and it seems its appearance is that of air, of rain,
that time, something with wave and wings, passes by,
grows. And the harp awakes from oblivion.

Theater of the Gods

It is like this on the coast.
Suddenly, contorted,
harsh, piled up,
static,
collapsing,
either tenacious theaters,
or ships and corridors
or rolling
severed limbs:
it is like this on the coast,
the rocky lunar slope,
the grapes of granite.

Orange stains
of oxide, green seams,
above the chalky peace,
that the seafoam strikes with its keys
or dawn with its rose
these stones are like this:
no one knows
if they came from the sea or will return to the sea,
something
astonished them
while they lived,
and they faltered in the stillness
and constructed a dead city.

A city without cries,
without kitchens,

a solemn ring
of purity,
tumbling pure shapes
in a confusion without resurrection,
in a crowd that lost its vision,
in a grey monastery condemned
to the naked truth of its gods.

The Lion

A great lion arrived from afar:
it was huge as silence,
it was thirsty, seeking blood,
and behind his investiture,
he had fire like a house,
it burned like a mountain of Osorno.

It found only solitude.
It roared of shyness and hunger:
it could eat only air,
seafoam unpunished by the coast,
frozen sea lettuce,
breeze the color of birds,
unappealing nourishment.

Melancholy lion from another planet
cast up by the high tide
to the small rocky islands of Isla Negra,
the salty archipelago,
with no more than an empty snout,
idle claws
and a tail of ragged feathers.

It felt all the ridicule
of its warlike appearance
and with the passing years
it wrinkled in shame.
Its fear then brought on
the worst arrogance

and it went on growing old like one
of the lions in the plaza,
it transformed into an ornament
for a stone staircase or garden,
until it buried its sad forehead,
fixed its eyes on the rain,
and remained quiet hoping for
the grey justice of stone,
its geologic hour.

I Will Return

Some other time, man or woman, traveler,
later, when I am not alive,
look here, look for me
between stone and ocean,
in the light storming
through the foam.
Look here, look for me,
for here I will return, without saying a thing,
without voice, without mouth, pure,
here I will return to be the churning
of the water, of
its unbroken heart,
here, I will be discovered and lost:
here, I will, perhaps, be stone and silence.

The Great Stone Table

We arrive at the great stone table
the children of Lota, Quepe,
Quitratue and Metrenco.
Of Ranquilco, Selva Oscura,
Yumbel, Yungay and Osorno.

We sit by the table,
the cold table of the world
and no one has brought us anything.
Everything was consumed,
they had eaten all of it.

One plate alone remains,
waiting on the immense hard table
of the world and the void.
Still a child waits
who is the truth of every dream,
who is the hope of our earth.

Where the Thirsty Fell

Hips of stone in the desert.

Here the walker fell
on death.
Here ended the journey
and the traveler.
Everything was sun, everything was thirst and sand.
He couldn't stand it and became silent.

Then came the next one
and he greeted
the fallen one
with a stone,
with a thirsty stone from the road.

Oh heart of scattered dust,
transformed into desert dust,
traveler and companion heart,
perhaps, of nitrate mines and works,
perhaps of the bitter mining,
you left and took to the road in the sand,
by the desert salt, with the sand.

Now a stone and another
erected here
a monument to the tired hero,
who couldn't stand it and abandoned his two feet,
then his legs, then his gaze,
life on the road of sand.

Now a stone came,
a harsh memory flew,
a smooth stone arrived,
and the tomb of the man in the desert
is a fist of solidarity in stone.

The Portrait in the Rock

Yes, I knew him, I lived years
with him, with his substance of gold and stone.
He was a man who was worn down.
In Paraguay he left his father and mother,
his sons, his nephews,
his latest in-laws,
his gate, his hens
and some half-opened books.
They called him to the door.
When he opened it, the police took him
and they beat him so much
that he spat blood in France, in Denmark,
in Spain, in Italy, traveling,
and so he died and I stopped seeing his face,
stopped hearing his profound silence.
Then once, on a stormy night,
with snow weaving
a pure coat on the mountains,
a horse, there, in the distance,
I looked and there was my friend:
his face was formed in stone,
his profile defied the wild weather,
in his nose the wind was muffling
the howls of the persecuted.
There the man driven from his land returned:
here in his country, he lives, transformed into stone.

The Ship

We walked and climbed: the world
was a parched noon,
the air didn't tremble, the leaves didn't exist,
the water was far away.

The boat or prow then
rose from the deserts
and sailed toward the sky:
a point of stone guided
toward the unbearable infinity,
a closed palace
for the lost gods.
And there was the prow, the arrow, the ship
or dreadful tower,
and for the toiling,
the thirsty, the dusty,
the sweating race
of man that climbed
the difficult hills,
neither water nor bread nor pasture,
only a large rock that rose,
only a stubborn boat of stone and music.

For how long? I cried out, we shouted.
Finally mother earth killed us
with its harsh cactus,
with its ironous maternity,
with all this desert,
sweat, wind and sand,

and when we finally arrived
to rest, wrapped in void,
a boat of stone
still wanted to ship us
toward where, without wings,
we couldn't fly
without dying.

This we endured when we were tired
and the mountain range was hard,
heavy as a chain.

Only then, my journey ended, here:
beyond, where death began.

The Rugged Ship

Boat of thorns
pierced
like the breast of a man
in a voyage of pain,
banner
that pierced
time
with its struggle
and later
waving in and out, left in the cracks
the chalky winter,
snow,
snow of stone,
snow of mad and solitary stone,
then
the cactus of the Pacific
deposited its nests,
its electric hair of thorns.
And the wind loved this immovable
ship and flying swiftly
it granted its treasures:
the beard of the islands,
a cold whisper,
changed into a honeycomb for eagles,
and asked for its sails
so that the sea could feel
the pure stone passing from wave to wave.

The Creation

That happened in the great silence
when grass was born,
when light had just detached itself
and created the vermilion and the statues,
then
in the great solitude
a howl began,
something rolled crying,
the shadows half-opened, rising alone
as if the planets sobbed
and then the echo
rolled, tumbling and tumbling
until what was born was silent.

But stone preserved the memory.

It guarded the opened snout of the shadows,
the trembling sword of the howl,
and there is in the stone an animal without name
that still howls without voice toward the emptiness.

The Tomb of Victor Hugo on Isla Negra

One stone among all,
smooth gravestone,
undisturbed like the proportion
of a planet
here in the solitudes
it was ordained,
and the waves lap at it,
the seafoam washes it,
but it emerges
smooth, imposing, clear,
among the rugged and hard rocks,
round and serene,
oval, resolute
by majestic dead
and no one knows who sleeps surrounded
by the unfathomable coastal fury,
no one knows, only
the albatross moon,
the cross of the cormorant, the firm leg
of the pelican, only the
sea knows it, only the
sad green thunder of dawn.

Silence, sea! Hushed
the seafoam recites the lord's prayer,
extends its long seaweed hair,
its humid cry
extinguishes
the seagull:

here lies the grave,
here finally woven
for a craggy mounument hurling
its song to cover itself with whiteness
of the incessant sea and its labors,
and buried in the earth,
in the fragrance
of France cool and subtle
sailing its matter,
surrendering to the sea its submerged beard,
crossing latitudes,
searching among the currents,
passing through typhoons and hips
of pure archipelagoes,
until the torrential doves
of the South Sea of Chile,
attracted the tricolored steps
of the snowy phantom
and here it rests, alone
and liberated:
entering the turbulent light,
kissed by salt and storm,
and father of its own eternity
sleeping finally, outstretched,
reclining in the intermittent thunder,
at the end of the sea and its cascades,
in the sails of its own power.

The Three Ducklings

A thousand
times
a thousand
years ago
plus one
a bright duckling flew
over the sea.
He went to discover the islands.
He wanted to talk
with the fan
of the palm tree,
with the leaves of the banana, to eat
the tricolored seeds
of the archipelago,
to be married
and establish
hemispheres populated
by ducks.
In the wild springs
he wanted
to establish lagoons
dignified with day lilies.
He was an exotic duck
to be
lost
in the middle
of the foamy
thickets of Chile.

When
he flew
like an arrow
his two brothers
cried
tears
of stone.

He heard them
fall
in his flight,
in the middle of the circle
of water,
in the central
navel
of the great ocean
and he returned.

But
his brothers
were
now
only
two obscure
stones
of granite,
since
each tear turned
into stone:
the weeping
without measure
petrified

the pain
into a monument.

Then, the wandering
repentant
huddled together his wings
and his dreams,
slept with his
brothers
and slowly the sea,
salt,
and sky,
imprisoned him in his shivering
until he was again
a duck of stone.

And now
like
three
ships
sailing,
three ducks
in time.

The Turtle

The turtle that
has walked
so long   ∗
and seen so much
with
his
ancient
eyes,
the turtle
that fed on
olives
of the deep
sea,
the turtle that has swum
for seven centuries
and known
seven
thousand
springs,
the turtle
shielded
against
the heat
and cold,
against
the rays and waves,
the turtle
of yellow
and silver,

with stern
amber
spots
and rapine feet,
the turtle
remains
here
asleep,
and doesn't know it.

The old man
assumed
a hardness,
abandoned
the love of waves
and became rigid
as an iron plate.
Closing
the eyes that
have dared
so much
ocean, sky, time and earth,
and now, he sleeps
among the other
rocks.

The Heart of Stone

Look,
this
was the heart
of a siren.
Helplessly
hard
she came to the shores
to comb her hair
and play a game of cards.
Swearing
and spitting
among the seaweed.
She was the image
herself
of those
hellish
barmaids
that
in stories
murdered
the weary traveler.

She killed her lovers
and danced
in the waves.

And so,
time passed in
the wicked

life of the siren
until
her fierce
lover, the sailor
pursued her
with harpoon and guitar
through all the seafoam,
farther
than the most
distant archipelagoes,
and when
she reclined
in his arms,
the sailor
gave her
his beveled point,
a final kiss
and a justified death.

Then, from the ship
the dead
commanders
descended,
beheaded
by
that
treacherous
siren,
and with cutlass,
sword,
fork
and knife,

pulled out
the heart of stone
from her chest,
and, near the sea,
it was allowed
to anchor,
in order that
it could teach
the little
sirens
to learn
to behave
properly
with
the
enamored
sailors.

Air in the Stone

On the naked cliff
and in the hair
air
of rock and wave.
All changing skin hour by hour.
The salt becomes brine-soaked light,
the sea opens
its clouds,
and the sky
hurls green foam.
The brilliant day
is like a flower
driven into
a golden lance.
All
is
bell, cup,
emptiness, raising
the transparent heart
of stone
and
water.

To a Wrinkled Boulder

A wrinkled stone
polished
by sea, by air,
by time.
A giant rock, shaken
by a cyclone, by a volcano,
by a night
of seafoam and black guitars.

Only a
royal
stone
in the middle
of time and earth,
triumph
of immovability, of harshness,
majestic like the stars
facing
all
that stirs,
alone
profound, dense and pure.

Oh solitary statue
rising
from the sand!
Oh naked bulk
where ash-colored
lizards climb,

that drink
a goblet
of dew
in the dawn,
stone
against seafoam,
against changing sky,
against spring.

Infinite stone erected by
the pure hands of solitude
in the middle of the sand!

The Stones and the Birds

Birds of the South Sea,
resting,
it is the hour
of great solitude, the hour of stone.
I knew every nest,
the unsociable lodging
of the nomadic,
I loved your Antarctic flight,
the somber accuracy of the remote birds.

Now, rest
in the amphitheater
of the islands:
no longer can I
talk with you,
there are no
            letters, there is no
                        telegraph
between poet and bird:
there is secret music,
only hidden wings,
plumage and power.

How much distance and greed
awaited the cruel gold eyes
of the silver fugitive!

With closed wings
a meteor descended,

exploding in your seafoam light,
and the flight again ascended,
climbing to the heights with a bloody fish.

From the Chilean Archipelago,
there, where rain
established its home,
great black wings
came cutting the sky,
and dominating
the territories and distances
of winter,
here on the continent
of solitary stone,
love, manure, life,
all that is left,
adventurous birds
of stone, sea and impossible sky.

To the Traveler

These stones aren't sad.
Within them lives gold,
they have the seeds of planets,
they have bells in their depths,
gloves of iron, marriages
of time with the amethysts:
on the inside laughing with rubies,
nourishing themselves from lightning.

Because of this, traveler, pay attention
to the hardships of the road,
to mysteries on the walls.

I know this at great cost,
that all life is not outward
nor all death within,
and that the age writes letters
with water and stone for no one,
so that no one knows,
so that no one understands anything.

The Tender Bulk

Don't be frightened by the relentless face
that earthquakes and bad weather
have carved, sea grasses,
small plants the color of a
                star
raised by the stubborn neck
of the defiant mountain.

The impulse, the ecstasy, the anger,
stayed within the stone,
and when the form exploded
into the planets,
earthly plants flowered
in its wrinkles of granite
and a tenderness remained.

Bird

The bird, bird, bird:
bird, flying, bird,
escape to your nest, climb to the sky,
peck the clouds of water,
cross the full moon,
the brilliant sun and the distances
with your plumage of basalt
and your abdomen of stone feathers.

Stones for Maria

The pure pebbles,
oval olives,
were once
inhabitants
of the ocean's
vines,
clusters
of grapes
in submerged honeycombs:
The waves picked them,
felled by wind,
rolling in the abyss
among slow-moving fish
and sleepwalking jellyfish,
tails of lacerated sharks,
eels like bullets!
Transparent stones,
smooth stones,
pebbles,
sliding toward
the bottom of humid regions,
far below, near where
the sky reemerges
and the sea dies above its artichokes.

Rolling and rolling
among the fingers and lips underwater
down to the smooth interminable,
until they were only touch,

curve of the smooth cup,
petal of the hip.
Then the surf grew stronger
and a beat of hard wave,
a hand of stone
winnowed cobbles
sifted them along the coast
and then disappeared in silence:
small amber teeth,
raisins of honey and salt, beans of water,
blue olives of the wave,
forgotten almonds in the sand.

Stones for Maria!
Stones of honor for her labyrinth!

She, like a spider
of transparent stone,
will weave her embroidery,
make her banner of pure stone,
fabricate, with silvery stones,
the structure of the day;
with sulfurous stones,
the root of a lost lightning flash,
and one by one will climb to her wall,
to the pattern, to the honesty, to the motion,
the fugitive stone,
the grape of the sea has returned to the clusters
wearing the light of her seafoam full of wonder.

Stones for Maria!

Wrinkled agates of Isla Negra,
sulfurous stones
of Tocopilla, like shattered stars,
decending from hellish mineral,
stones of La Serenta that the ocean
smoothed and then settled in the heights,
and from Coquimbo the black power,
the rolling basalt
of Maitencillo, of Tolten, of Niebla,
the wet dress
of the Chiloe seashore,
round stones, stones like eggs
of southern birds, translucent fingers
of the secret salt, of frozen
quartz, or enduring heritage
of the Andes, boats
and monasteries
of granite.

Praise
the stones
of Maria,
those that she arranged like a crystal bee
in the honeycomb of her wisdom:
the stones
of its walls,
of the book that is built
letter by letter,
leaf by leaf,
and stone by stone!
It is necessary to see and read this beauty
and I love its hands

from whose power
appears, gently,
a
lesson
of stone.

Antarctic Stones

There all ends
and doesn't end:
there all begins:
rivers and ice part,
air is married to snow,
there are no streets or horses
and the only building
stone built.
No one inhabits the castle
not even the lost souls
that the cold and frigid wind
frightened:
the solitude of the world alone is there
and so the stone
became music,
lifting its slender heights,
raising itself to cry or sing
but it remained silent.
Only the wind, the whip
of the South Pole, whistled,
only the white void
and a noise of rain birds
around the castle of solitude.

Nothing More

I stood by truth:
to establish light in the land.

I wanted to be common like bread:
so when the struggle came she wouldn't find me missing.

But here I am with what I loved,
with the solitude I lost:
but by this stone I don't rest.

The sea works in my silence.

SEAQUAKE

TRANSLATED BY
MARIA JACKETTI & DENNIS MALONEY

Seaquake

The clocks of the sea,
the artichokes,
the blazing money boxes,
the pockets of the sea
full of hands,
the lamps of water,
the shoes and boots
of the ocean,
the mollusks, the sea cucumbers,
the defiant crabs,
certain fish that swim and sigh,
the sea urchins that exit,
the deep sea's chestnuts,
the ocean's azure umbrellas,
the broken telegrams,
the waltz over the waves,
the seaquake gives all of this to me.

The waves returned to the Bible:
page by page the water closed:
all anger returned to the sea's center,
but between my eyes what remains
are the varied and useless treasures
that the sea left me, the ocean's dismantled love
and shadowy rose.

Touch this harvest:
here my hands worked
the diminutive tombs of salt
destined for being and substances,

ferocious in their livid beauty
in their limestone stigmas,
fugitives,
because they will feed us
and other beings
with so much flowering and devouring light.

What the seaquake left at the door,
the fragile force, the submarine eye,
the blind animals of the wave,
push me into the conflict,
Come! And come! Bid farewell! Oh tempest,
to my tide hidden by the sea.

Cockles spilled on the sand,
slippery arms,
stomachs of water,
armor open at the entrance
of the repetition and the movement,
quills, suction cups, tongues,
little cold bodies,
abused
by the implacable eternity of water,
by the wind's anger.

Here, being and not being were combined
in radiant and hungry structures:
life burns and death passes,
like a flash of lightning.
I am the only witness
to the electricity and the splendor
that fills the devouring calmness.

The Picoroco

The picoroco imprisoned
in a terrible tower,
extends a blue claw, palpitates,
desperate in the storm.

The picoroco is tender inside its tower:
white as flour of the sea
but no one can reach the secret
of its cold gothic castle.

*Picoroco–A Chilean shellfish

Seaweed

I am the seaweed of the storm
dashed by the surf:
the stirrings of shipwrecks
and the storm's hands
moved and instructed me:
here you have my cold flowers,
my simulated submission
to the wind's judgment:
I survive the water,
the salt, the fishermen,
with my elastic latitude,
and my vestments of iodine.

The Sea Urchin

The sea urchin is the sun of the sea,
centrifugal and orange,
full of quills like flames,
made of eggs and iodine.

The sea urchin is like the world:
round, fragile, hidden:
wet, secret, and hostile:
the sea urchin is like love.

Starfish

When the stars in the sky
ignore the firmament
and go off to sleep by day,
the stars of the water greet
the sky buried in the sea
inaugurating the duties
of the new undersea heavens.

Shells

Empty shells of the sand,
that the sea abandoned when it receded,
when the sea left to travel,
to travel through other seas.

The ocean cast off sea shells
polished by its mastery,
whitened by so many kisses
from the waves that left to travel.

Crayfish

Stop! Casual leopards
of the seashore, curved
assailants like rosy swords
from the undersea roughness,
all biting at the same time,
undulating like fever
until they all tumble into the net
and exit dressed in blue
destined for scarlet catastrophe.

Conch Shell

The conch shell awaits the wind
asleep in the sea's light:
it wants a black-colored voice
that may fill all the distances
like the piano of the powerful,
like God's horn
for the scholarly books:
it wants to blow away their silence
until the sea immobilizes
their bitter insistence of lead.

Seal

The knot of zoology
is this functional seal
that lives in a sack of rubber
or inside the black light of its skin.

Inside of her,
inherent movements circulate
to the sea's kingdom
and one sees this enclosed being
in the storm's gymnasium,
discovering the world encircled
by staircases of ice,
until she gazes at us with
the planet's most penetrating eyes.

Sea Anenome

The flower of the salty boulder
opens and cancels its crown
by the will of salt
with water's appetite.

Oh corolla of cold flesh
and vibrating pistils,
widow-anenome, intestine.

Jaiva

The violet-colored crab
lurks in the corner of the sea:
its pincers are the two enigmas:
its appetite is an abyss.

Later its armor agonizes
in a hellish bowl
and now it is nothing more than a rose:
the delectable red rose.

The Bronze Dolphin

If the dolphin fell into the sea
it would sink to the bottom, plummet
with its yellow weight.

Among true fish
it would be a foreign object,
a fish without soul, without language

until the sea would devour it,
gnawing on its bronze pride,
converting it into sand.

Octopus

Octopus, oh blood-colored monk,
the fluttering of your robe
circulates on the salt of the rock
like a satanic slickness.
Oh visceral testimony,
branch of congealed rays,
monarchy's head
of arms and premonitions:
portrait of the chill,
plural cloud of black rain.

Sun of the Sea

One day at Isla Negra I found
a sun sleeping in the sand,
a centrifugal and central sun
covered with fingers of gold
and windswept needles.

I picked up the sandy sun
and raised it to the light,
comparing it to the sun in the sky.

They didn't see each other.

Swordfish

Two marine swordfish
guard the gate of the sea.
They fling it aside
They bring the tide
They fling it wide.

The swordfish are from Iquique,
from the blue ocean
that reaches Vladivostock
and swells at my feet.

The swordfish sentinels
with swords lengthwise
close the door of the sea
and prepare to keep watch
so order doesn't enter
the ocean's chaos.

Fish Market

Fish hang by their tails,
the spilled fish shine,
the fish display their silver,
even the crabs still threaten.
On the huge decorated table,
through the submarine scales,
only the body of the sea is missing.
It does not die; it is not for sale.

Farewell to the Offerings of the Sea

Return, return to the sea
from these pages!

Fishes, mollusks, seaweed,
escapees from the cold,
return to the waist
of the Pacific,
to the giddy kiss
of the wave, to the secret
logic of rock.

Oh hidden ones,
naked ones, submerged ones,
slippery ones,
it is the time
of division and separation:
paper reclaims me,
the ink, the inkwells,
the printing presses, the letters,
the illustrations,
the characters and numbers
jumbled in riverbeds from
where
they ambush me: the women,
and the men
want my love, ask for my company,
the children from Petorca,
from Atacama, from Arauco,
from Loncoche,

also want to play with the poet!

A train waits for me, a ship
loaded with apples,
an airplane, a plough,
some thorns.
Goodbye, harvested
fruits of the water, farewell,
imperially dressed
shrimps,
I will return, we will return
to the unity
now interrupted.
I belong to the sand:
I will return to the round sea
and to its flora
and to its fury:
but for now—I'll wander
whistling
through the streets.

THE AUTHOR

Pablo Neruda (1904–1973) is regarded as the greatest Latin American poet of the 20th century. The breadth, vision, and range of themes in his work are extraordinary. Born in the coastal town of Temuco in southern Chile, he moved to the capital, Santiago, in 1921. His first book was published in 1923, and the next year saw the publication of his famous collection, *Twenty Poems of Love and One Song of Despair*. During the 1920s and 30s, he served as a diplomat in various locations, culminating with an appointment as ambassador to Spain in 1934. These years of poetic and political development were shattered by the outbreak of the Spanish Civil War in 1936. Neruda's poetic style shifted significantly to address the social and political concerns of the war. The result was his collection, *Spain in My Heart*. He returned to Chile in 1938 and began construction of his house at Isla Negra, where he lived, except for periods of exile, until his death in 1973. The poems in this volume reflect his life at Isla Negra and are taken from three collections: *A House in the Sand (Una casa en la arena*, 1966*), The Stones of Chile (Las piedras de Chile*, 1961*)*, and *Seaquake (Maremoto*, 1969*)*. Pablo Neruda won the Nobel Prize in 1971.

THE TRANSLATORS

Maria Jacketti is a poet, fiction writer, and translator. She teaches at St. Peter's College in New Jersey. Her other books of translation include *A Gabriela Mistral Reader* and three books by Pablo Neruda: *Heaven Stones*, *Neruda's Garden: An Anthology of Odes*, and *Ceremonial Songs*.

Dennis Maloney is a poet, translator, and landscape architect. His other books of translation include *The Landscape of Soria* by Antonio Machado, *Naked Woman* by Juan Ramon Jimenez, *Between the Floating Mist: Poems of Ryokan* and *Tangled Hair: Poems of Yosano Akiko*. Several volumes of his own poetry have been published, including *The Map is Not the Territory*.

Clark M. Zlotchew is a writer, translator, and professor of Spanish at the State University of New York College at Fredonia. His translations include *Seven Conversations with Jorge Luis Borges* and *Falling Through the Cracks*, stories by Julio Ricci.